Later in Chicago

*Dedicated to my daughter
Kathleen Forsythe*

Later in Chicago

by
Fred Cogswell

Borealis Press
Ottawa, Canada
2003

Copyright © by Fred Cogswell
and Borealis Press Ltd., 2003

*All rights reserved. No part of this book may
be used or reproduced in any manner whatsoever without
written permission except in the case of brief quotations
embodied in critical articles and reviews.*

Canada

*The Publishers acknowledge the financial support
of the Government of Canada through the Book Publishing
Industry Development Program (BPIDP)
for our publishing activities*

National Library of Canada Cataloguing in Publication Data

Cogswell, Fred, 1917-
    Later in Chicago / Fred Cogswell

Poems.
ISBN 0-88887-212-7

    I. Title.

PS8555.O3L38 2003   C811'.54   C2003-902360-5
PR9199.3.C56L38 2003

Cover design by Bull's Eye Design, Ottawa
Typesetting by Chisholm Communications, Ottawa

Printed and bound in Canada on acid-free paper

Contents

Preface ix

I. **Longer Poems** 1
   From Somewhere Else... 2
   Writer's Block 4
   Paradoxes 6
   Young Or Old 8
   Turnabouts 10
   A Confession 12
   Inside A Time-Locked Phrase... 14
   Advice 16
   For Any Life To Have Its Fullest Fling 18
   The Reason Why I Love Baseball 20
   Almost 22
   In The Great World Of Being 24
   A Stereotyped Confession 26
   Sentimentality 28
   The World Of Them And Us 30
   A Prophecy 32
   I Found The Hope: The Voice Of Dog 34
   If I Wished 36
   For More Than Seventy Years 38
   An Observation 40
   The One-Eyed Giant .42
   How Can I Say...? 43
   Black And White 44
   Two Sculptures 45
   Alone In A Forest 46
   Comma Butterfly 47
   At Times Sometimes .48
   Girls 49
   Wherever I Watch... 50
   To Form Sweet Notes 51

  Perhaps Too Fortunate, The Worm 52
  Film Review: The Fast Runner 53
  Two Fables 54
  Henry Adams At Chartres .55
  The Magic Tree 56

II. Incidentals 57
  Carmen 58
  A Tribute 58
  The Dress 58
  A Poem Is A Saw 59
  In The Mad World 59
  Once We Watched 59
  Seven Words 60
  I've Written Poems 60
  Reflections 60
  To A Friend 61
  Augustine 61
  Harriet Beecher Stowe 62
  Inside The Hollow Heart .62
  Divisive Walls 62
  De Sade 63
  First Time 63
  We Dig Beneath 64
  The Work Ethic 64
  The Dwarf Bonsai 64
  A Subject For Shame 65
  On The Beach 65
  If Brainless Apes 66
  Although The Past 66
  Without A Sound 66
  Assessment 67
  The World I Live In 67
  Now I Am Old 68
  Base-Lines On Marriage 68
  Noise 68

Our Curt Concern 69
  I, Unborn 69
  Dilemma 69
  Once The Pebbles On The Beach 70
  The Red Rose 70
  An Author's Name 70
  When Chance Rage 71
  The Broad Dark Street 71
  As Far As Answers Go 71
  Earth-Play (For Anti-Environmentalists) 72
  Although Words... 72
  The Sting 73
  Wind And Rain 73
  Brotherhood 73
  The Poetry Of Energy 74
  When I Re-Read My Poems 74
  Exposed Now To A Light 75
  Grammar Is Mainly Hit Or Miss 75
  The Lord Of The Rings 76
  Taste 76
  The Things Which Tell Me 77
  Fear 77
  Automatic Responses 78
  Once I Fashioned Verse 78

III. (Arranged from the French) 79
  Herodias (Théodore De Banville) 80
  To A Passer-By (Charles Baudelaire) 81
  Windows (Charles Beaudelaire) 82
  In Brown Limbs (Emile Blémont) 84
  Reflection (Joë Bousquet) 85
  A Bird (René Char) 85
  Landscape (Robert Desnos) 86
  Nothing Alarms Me More (Paul Éluard) 87
  Forbidden (Léonard Forest) 88
  An Unending Song (Léonard Forest) 91

Sonnet (Émile Goudreau)	94
Léda (Jean Lahor)	95
The Prairie (Charles Leconte De Lisle)	96
Pegasus (Pierre Lowÿs)	98
Song (Jean Moréas)	99
The Deep Life (Anna De Noailles)	100
The Four Elements (Géo Norge)	101
Late In Life (Pierre Reverdy)	102
Privilege (Claude Serret)	103
The Poetry Of The Street (Marcel Thiry)	104
Silent, Sleek, And Perfectly (Jean Tortel)	105
Pomegranates (Paul Valéry)	106
The Cry (Émile Verhaeren)	107
The Sky Is, Over The Roof (Paul Verlaine)	109
On The Earth (André Ferdinand Hérold)	110

Preface

I am not sure what his politics may be, and I doubt if at this point the matter is relevant. But it is relevant that, as an editor and critic, Cogswell has displayed a most admirable strain of radical Toryism which has enabled him to understand and recognize poets who find they can best express themselves in traditional ways at the same time as he has empathized freely with those who are by temperament experimental. Especially, through his Fiddlehead Books, he has made sure that many valid but unfashionable poets have had their day in print and that their words are available for us to read and perhaps for later critics to admire, as we today have come to admire at least some of the works of the poets who are here discussed. Our debt to Cogswell in this respect is considerable; virtually single-handedly, he has sustained through an era oriented towards experimentalism the traditional currents of poetry, and so he speaks with a peculiar authority when he defends these early poets, not by making an untenable claim for originality amounting to genius,... but by explaining and defending the derivativeness they shared, after all, with Shakespeare.

We have to note, as Cogswell says, "that those from whom Mair borrowed were likewise borrowers, that in fact the very function of any tradition is the availability of a past from which to draw, and that sociological and ideological changes in metropolitan life often produce even greater dislocations between form and content than those that occur in the colonies." ...[This] is perhaps the most important passage in Cogswell's essay on Mair, perhaps even the most important passage in this book, in which he defines the role of a traditional poetic in a still essentially conservative political and moral order:

"*Charles Mair was moved to write poetry by his reading of the work of other poets—the great masters of the past and the more popular poets of his own time. To all aspiring poets of that time, the world of poetry must have seemed a timeless world—one in which human nature was a constant, and a poetic diction one convention rather than a series of successive conventions. Certain phrases, similes, metaphors, in use for centuries, were considered as much a part of poetic equipment as the use of "thou" or "thee", of metrical forms and rhymes. Like human nature and poetic form and language, the purpose and the themes of poetry were thought of as constants. The purpose was to instruct and to entertain. By and large, the entertainment was thought to consist partly in the euphony of sound and shape produced by poetic form; partly in the delight of the reader in recognizing resemblances to and differences from other works in the work read; and, finally, in the quality of thought and imagination with which the theme was invested. Poetic themes embraced what exalted the human condition and either ignored or attacked what debased it."*

"Introduction," George Woodcock—
Canadian Writers And Their Works,
Poetry Series, Volume One
ECW Press, 1983

I.
Longer Poems

From Somewhere Else . . .

From somewhere else in another time
Something escaping is following me
Like a final ghost of a pantomime.
Its breath now echoes thought or deed maybe
That has not yet found possibility
But aches to become a part of my life.
I fear what it flees, and fear, too, the foe
Such a takeover will exact in strife.

From somewhere else in another time
Something escaping has crept close to me
So near now that its footsteps seem to chime
As they merge with my own steps hauntingly
Until I see and feel reality
As my twin in an almost double life,
But there at times they turn away and flee
And when they do it hurts like a knife.

From somewhere else in another time
Some thing escaping has joined life in me.
So close we care, sometimes we make one rhyme
And I have learned from this that to be free
Plays havoc with reliability
And carves up habit with a psychic knife.
I still am resolved to let this state be,
Content to form life-movement shaped by strife.

From somewhere else in another time
Something escaping I will not refuse.
If it can reach me in its lonely climb
I shall embrace it, let it be my Muse.

Writer's Block

At this moment, I, a writer, possess
Thousands of words, in a dictionary.
I read them one by one, find them useless
To melt together in one unity.
I open my mind-eye. Light I can't see
And I cannot even think of a form.
I completely lack polarity
With just my naked self to keep me warm.

At this moment, I wonder more than less
Whether the outer blindness now in me
Is Alzeimer's disease. The emptiness
And isolation and despondency
Joined with the lack of hopefulness can be
The frustration of the need to conform
That cannot find a form, the misery
Of the normlessness of every norm.

This makes me think of Emma Best,
A matron friend of my first family.
Who had Alzeimer's and who expressed
What it meant to her quite differently:
"They keep me here because I only see
Each person is an untapped uniform.
Now that I know this is true I can be
Myself in peace and not create a storm."

Prince, between a poet's view and Emma's
The difference is but a slight degree.
Altzeimer's . . . writer's block . . . both dilemmas
In the psyche's long struggle to be free.

Paradoxes

I let my life pursue its routine way,
In rites that repetitions harmonize,
Nor did I know until I woke today
How insidiously the body lies.
With brilliance that dazzles beyond surprise
The only name I have for light is "thrill".
Thanks to Doctor Brewer's fine laser skill
I am an old man but I have young eyes.

I let my thoughts pursue their routine way
From old books which others consider wise
And wear them, proud of their outside array,
Without concern for either shape or size
Until a touch that to my touch replies
Awakes the time-drugged earth I cannot kill.
Now caught in my own life-defying will
I'm an old man in a young exercise.

I know that sight and touch defy each day
And become incapable of surprise
Which memory and hope alone convey
By relativities of time and size.
In the moment's heart there can be no lies.
What's real is ever found beyond the will
As infinity being cannot kill
Is locked in ageless, spaceless exercise.

Good Prince, there is an irony at play
In which life and thought can never agree;
The words that we wrestle with night and day
Are too static to catch eternity.

Young Or Old

I love your face. It never fails to start
A vital force in me whose keenness stays
As intense as it is. It makes my heart
Pump blood through its labyrinthine ways.
Sometimes what it gives now will last for days.
Its sweetness is so much a song unsung
That each time my old eyes embrace your gaze
I always hope the touch will keep me young.

I love your face, but could I love your heart?
The blood it contains is more like a maze.
Motives are there but they unite and part
Often in very mysterious ways
And I am not equipped for yeas and nays.
For what I see I'm neither old nor young,
And as long as its silent music plays
I'll love your face although I fear your tongue.

I love your face. Your eyes more than your heart
Always must merit the most of my praise.
Like tiny swift swallows their air-paths part
Over this world's gross and soul-clogging ways.
The spirituality in their light-rays
Reminds me of the psychic reports of Jung,
The timeless myths and the magic of days
Destroying the meaning of old and young.

I love your face, but I long for release
From language, time, colour, sex, and size.
In a placeless place when I wish for peace
I know it is there, lady, in your eyes.

Turnabouts

Though germs and spores are more than numberless
And cancers in the body's blood appear,
Though hearts half broken up by homelessness
Linger through their living death year by year,
The greatest killer yet is human fear.
When men applied for cure, their doctors wrote:
"What use to treat? Though medicines are here,
Nothing that we know can be the antidote."

Harassed by the plagues which portrayed their stress
The people turned instinctively to get clear
Of a world they saw as a dying mess,
Seeking a timeless space and a spaceless year.
They said then: "Anywhere flesh can't appear
Is safe and sacred." Because of this they wrote:
"If bodies were erased there'd be no fear.
Flesh is men's disease. God is its antidote."

Though first in its newness their faith they blessed,
People were troubled again. Some saw clear
That the life they wanted was more than rest
And peace on an earth needs more to be here.
They brought the old world back, with it their fear.
Not long after this a new thinker wrote.
He let what he thought a new phrase appear:
"God is men's disease. Flesh is its antidote."

A Confession

I will not share the pangs of men
Who spend their time between carouse
And rage. Although such passions then
Can bring much madness to a mouse
I save my pity for a spouse
Whose strength of will I can't admire
Who tries to burn a burning house
In order to put out a fire.

I will not share the pangs of men
Nor will I, too, their work espouse.
That leaves only pity. When
I watch a hurt-divided house
I don't in grief my feelings souse
Nor laud the acts I can't admire.
The will in me won't rise to dowse
Any long-existent fire.

I watched the world of insects then.
Their hot energies don't keep vows
And feelings are more acute. When
A spider-web a victim cows
Being is not sweet. Pains arouse
The scattered sparks of vanished fire
On which their hungers have to browse.
Time ends the black that most desire.

In life I do not want to place
Confusion in the where and when.
Though worlds may change in time and place
One pattern stays. I call it zen.

Inside A Time-Locked Phrase . . .

Inside a time-locked phrase each word's a noose
That grips a literate posterity
Subject to the pressure of sound abuse
And the shifting winds of propriety
With power to blur its hard-won clarity.
This makes communication a leaning
Tower that catches winds of history,
The past, present future of all meaning.

Too much of the impact words that we use
Lie in context, tone, and the memory
Of sounds that go with them to make us choose
What best blends to form oral harmony.
Too seldom will the brain let one word be.
With any sentence there are convening
Elements to create a tapestry.
And only the minor parts are meaning,

In most situations our tongues let loose
To end a doubt or an uncertainty
By stating values where the choice we choose
(Presuming hearers are more deaf than we)
Is not in words but in velocity.
Rites are stronger. From them we are gleaning
A vision that can give their inanity
The united power of a screening.

Good Prince! Use the words that you wish to use
Nor care too much what all of them can be.
Take it for granted that thought is abstruse
And at least put an end to pedantry.

Advice

There are in life some laws that are not nice
Which in our souls we try to seek in vain.
Beneath the sacred myths of sacrifice
Our feelings hold their opposites in train.
Therefore what's been is bound to be again.
The deaths of Christian martyrs tell us this:
"Beyond the sharpest edge of human pain
Lies the possibility of bliss."

Day after day life's patient laws suffice
Though some in numbers new examples gain
And dreams create a world of fire and ice
Which on earth's patience puts atomic strain,
Such extremity goes beyond the grain.
The goal of life is never only bliss;
In any world life's highest wish is vain.
It comes by chance and ends in an abyss.

To feel is real. Where thought is just device
And hope may be an anodyne for pain
You must not let the things you think suffice.
Each by itself inflicts too great a strain.
Despite our ego's sense of might and main
The only end in life we have seems this:
"You die just once. You cannot die again.
Let accidents dissolve both pain and bliss."

For Any Life To Have Its Fullest Fling

For any life to have its fullest fling
And not miss out by aberration
We need to get and give everything,
Learn value where we find variation,
And from each encountered situation
Make a memory map out of each part
That will give ample accommodation
With psychic space for both the head and heart.

But when traffic models flow, speeding,
One is puzzled by the cooperation
Of cars that zing and pause and pause and zing
Till red and green find their termination.
How does this happen? Is there anyone
Who really knows whether our human part
Or the machine determines what goes on?
Perhaps it's something outside head and heart.

It is most likely, caught in traffic's fling
We are convinced that acceleration
Is our own will and not our engine's spring
And that the road through which our bodies run
Is part of a huge map aeons old, begun
When everything that is had its start.
We may be dots that move mapped illusion
For which each credits his own head and heart.

Prince, on the map all selfhood's a mistake.
The whole is always greater than the part,
And the mighty world which world movements make
Is bigger, longer than all head and heart.

The Reason Why I Love Baseball

The reason why I love baseball
Is because few games that I see
Offer up perfection at all.
I'm convinced inconsistency
Is athletes' deadly enemy
And I am glad. Were all complete
And played as they were meant to be
Suspense would be dull and not sweet.

The reason why I love baseball
Is how grounders bounce awkwardly
Or a sacrifice bunt dies in the tall
Grass, setting fast runners free
To reprieve their lost liberty.
Best of all, surprise most sweet,
When a gale-blast blows suddenly
To turn victory to defeat.

The reason why I love baseball
Is pressure that takes hold of me
Because of an umpire's wrong call
Which adds where it should never be
A wild note of morality
That is messy and never neat,
An extraneous thing that may be key
And turn victory to defeat.

I'm glad to have this game today:
Caught between "will be" and "what's been";
Now I can watch the cosmic play
Twixt the worlds of Yang and Yin.

Almost

The word that's most constantly used in speech
For the best things men and women do
Implies the failure of our human reach
Is somehow tied to shortness of the view.
The word "success" is limited to few
But what we say to elevate a boast
Is a word no logic can prove untrue
What man in what tongue has not said "almost"?

In endless games can the parts played by each
Be justly measured by a present's view?
Being may be such a game. In it reach
And grasp as passing points may make one view
Sometimes. Coincidence can't make them true
Forever. What others do is the ghost
We wish for inside our own milieu.
What man in what tongue has not said "almost"?

"Almost", like lye, can be in acid bleach
That latches on all doings, eats them through
And leaves them, bare white bones on a beach,
More static than unreliable glue.
If this is true, reader, what should you do?
Be blind and still and let your psyche roast
Or play all games as though each game were new?
On no account employ the word "almost".

I think poets should practise what they preach.
The nearest thing to truth here may be "almost";
But since the title much exceeds its reach,
Of this poem I shall not ever boast.

In The Great World Of Being

In the great world of being
Every wish is a prayer
And what's desire's seeing
Is accomplished somewhere;
For this let each beware.
Though right or wrong may dance
On things for which we care
Life's god is circumstance.

In the great world of being
Happenings everywhere
Rely on more than seeing
And on much more than care.
Whatever oaths we swear
By will or act or chance
Can make our control despair.
Life's god is circumstance.

In the great world of being
All things are. We can share
Or not what we're seeing,
Bear or not what we bear.
Feed love, hate, hope, despair.
But never rule the dance.
In our world everywhere
Life's god is circumstance.

Great Prince, form of being,
Look at all pride askance.
What we see is seeming.
Life's god is circumstance.

A Stereotyped Confession

I grew up in a code that kept
Me even from shedding my tears,
So strong it was I never wept
At all in my earlier years
But hid each sign that hinted fears.
It was the same way, too, with pain.
Wherever nerves are pierced with spears
No man should let himself complain.

But thus unused, some feelings slept.
This helped me marshal slow arrears
Until at last with ease I kept
The strong approval of my peers
Although not blind to women's fears
What things I felt I would not gain.
Wherever eyes dissolve in tears
No man should let himself complain.

What in youth I did not accept
In my old age at last appears
As feelings that too long have crept
Avoided for too many years
Revive my long unnoticed fears
To whip my soul like acid rain.
Though words for this are in arrears
I'm too much a man to complain.

I grew up in a code that kept
My strengths from pain and softness free.
Old now, I know too long have slept
Words in what's woman yet in me.

Sentimentality

Though sorrow for myself I scarcely feel
The woes of others often ache inside
And form mind-wounds whose scars are slow to heal
That I cannot cry for because of pride.
I hate the me which my best friends deride
When I explain my feelings honestly.
If I said today, "My poor dog has died,"
They would call it sentimentality.

Though sorrow for myself I scarcely feel
I pine for days that long ago have died.
The girls I only read about seem real
As if I now were walking by their side.
I can respond to scenes I never tried
And say what people did and said to me
But if I told them what I felt inside
They would call it sentimentality.

Though outside worlds say thought is most unreal
I still must love the world I own inside,
And though my inner self is not ideal
I can't ignore the much too-thick divide
That pits dimensions which could be world-wide
Against what's mine. If with this you don't agree
Because I love at once to think and feel
You can call it sentimentality.

Though sorrow for myself I scarcely feel
There'd be nothing better in the world at all
Than to co-exist on every keel
Without the dead barrier of a wall.

The World Of Them And Us

Although the world of them and us
Can be an apple cut in two,
Ins and outs there are curious.
The truth in what we think and do
Can't be much more than quarter-true,
How tight or loose is a language?
What light demands a darker hue?
What sun uncharged will last through age?

Although the world of them and us
Is dependent on a right eye-view
I think it would be ridiculous
To trust what left eye sees is you.
Twixt in and out there is no cue
And left and right no way presage
What it is you may run into.
Years of youth are not years of age.

Although the world of them and us
Possesses intuitions, too,
The psyches in it fume and fuss
And know not what they ought to do.
When actors reach the pitch they woo
Their dizzy height cannot assuage
The ignorance that turned them blue
Or made their fat minds feel flesh age.

Great Prince, if all of them and us
Shone bright upon your psyche's pad
Would truth grin there ridiculous
Or clear enough to make you mad?

A Prophecy

All objects which are newly found or rare
Can become a collector's world indeed.
A youthful view may find them anywhere
And look for things which old folk do not heed.
When wise eyes wear the glasses of a creed
Too long and keep them on, how can the lens
Be clear and bright? The logic of this screed
Invokes both plain and biblical amens.

The choice we made twixt either crop or tare
Has not been itemized in nature's creed.
Though it was not the faith by which men swear
The worms of earth are not the devil's seed
Nor do God's sun-rays spawn the sky's blue breed.
Dismiss such thoughts or simply call them yens.
There'll be much fewer books for us to read
And more trees left to breathe out still amens.

This present world has thrown so great a scare
On us, we let all human hopes recede.
Machine, robot, and clone are items there
Today in minds whose standardizations lead
Them to a brave new world not made in men's
Or women's images but in an iron creed
Where moving things have dirty oil to bleed
And automatic horns to honk amens.

Great Prince, I know this view has limited
Both alternatives that we wish to trust:
God's voice is grace's lack inhibited,
And Satan will have to make metal rust.

I Found The Hope: The Voice Of Dog

I found the hope the forefathers gave
Was much too narrow and too high.
It shamed me for the life I live
And made me too afraid to die.
I did not see it in the sky
Or earth, but in my doggy clay
I heard another voice reply.
That voice I hate but must obey.

My ear's a dog's ear too restive
To miss the echoes of a sky
Whose thin voice seeps through a mind-sieve
As dry as air too cold to die.
All those who hear it can't comply.
With whispered tongues too weak to say
They quite ignore the reason why.
There is no choice twixt nay and yea.

I look at hope which cannot live
Forefathers' faithful dog am I.
The food I eat is too costive
And water-springs are mostly dry.
Though existence is in supply
And time drags on from day to day
I wish the dog in me would die,
Eliminating yea and nay.

Good Prince, I know where magic dwells
Coincidence must stake a claim.
Beware the word whose order spells
The mirror-image of my name.

If I Wished

If I wished I know I could make a list
Of all the sweet things I've got from Nature
That I paid for by the pain she gave back.
At first I thought it longer than I wished,
But some offences there seemed only slight
Compared to Nature's strong and adverse account.

When I thought this first, it seemed "account"
Was sacrilege and that even "a list"
Was enough to pour at least a slight
On the generosity of Nature
That gave me all the things my wonder wished
And somehow never asked for something back.

Now I know that Nature can turn her back,
I shall draw upon my own will to count
Times when she has not given what I wished,
Half-hoping as I do that for the list
Which can end all my dealings with Nature
The total cost of payment will be slight.

Though the total cost of payment may be slight.
Old age is not the best time to pay back
An old account. The deal I have with Nature
Because it is a deal, will make a count
Dried out at last to just a barren list
That both my soul and body never wished.

Although I thought me honest and never wished
To own whatever was that gave delight,
Differences (which I could no way list
Because I knew not what they were) broke the back
Of what I thought to be a good account.
All the business I had with Nature.

Now I know I have not learned from Nature
Whose good news did not consult my wishes.
For scattered wealth too rich for men to count
In a one-way deal, waste is seldom slight.
A lesser waste would be to pay her back
And in any fight on her side enlist.

For More Than Seventy Years

For more than seventy years I wrote verse.
I took its forms from other works I read.
For my word-choice I used a lexicon
And seldom thought of what is uncommon
My images, too, lacked variety
Though I wrote about things I knew and saw.

When they read my poems, the critics saw
Basic banality within my verse
Which, joined with too little variety,
Was very commonplace for them to read,
And in their reviews the prime word "common"
Suited a prejudicial lexicon.

But when I read music, a lexicon
Used notes for words and in them there I saw
That common sounds need not be uncommon.
The self-same efforts could succeed in verse
As songs brought back fresh charms to those who read.
Repeated beats don't require variety.

Beats repeated don't require variety
And meaning's more than a word-lexicon.
The feeling sense of what your readers read
Brings back greater depth to thoughts you saw;
The pulse that drives blood-urges through all verse
Can change what's common to what's uncommon.

But no matter whether the word "common"
Applies, or else the word "variety"
Music can be identical with verse,
But if it's there, although no lexicon
Can word exactly everything I saw
It may become real truth to those who read.

It still becomes real truth to those who read
For though to me who wrote it it was common
Quite different truths in it the readers saw.
When it comes to judging variety
Each one himself becomes a lexicon.
This is the true miracle of verse.

The variety which most verse-readers saw
Can make the common become uncommon
And to more than words act as lexicon.

An Observation

Against the beach, the waves, too weak to pound,
Lap salt water too heavily for play
As tiny circles move a surface where
The strong dogs splash and tanned dark children wade.
No clouds remain to dim a summer sky
Where blue dissolves itself in cool clear light.

It has been said we love too much the light.
But since men saw which philosophies exposed
That god's best paradise is in the sky
They've loved the stars that twinkle in their play
And watched the moon in cloud-bogs wade.
Through what they thought, faith told them, what
    and where.

The wind of seeing faith is everywhere.
It blows in darkness, blows still more in light
And is by our imagination swayed.
It can with ignorance desire compound
And in our minds inject the glossy play
Which makes new life adorn our inner sky.

There was less room where then it put the sky
And time could never make out anywhere
The weight of what was there in play.
Inside the brain the quality of light
Could not be measured pound by pound
No matter by what method it was weighed.

No matter by what method it was weighed
The mind's grip was a prison for the sky
But the key to open it brain never found,
And though in and out eyes looked everywhere
They failed to find the liberty of light
And thought sky-gods were only just display.

It's time men looked to find another play
And catch the core of darkness in their train.
Although it was more gross than any light
It held as well as earth half of a sky.
It seemed full of diamonds and everywhere
Great gold which could be measured by the pound.

Our faiths in dark or light at best compound
Toil's long wear. As of now, our efforts strain.
We don't know the why nor what when we weigh.

THE ONE-EYED GIANT

In the world of our earth's fold
We seldom naked have to bear
The one-eyed giant's gaze of gold.

Sun-power here is so controlled
By cloud and wind and rain and air
In the world of our own earth's fold

That opposites, like heat and cold,
Form lids to soften in its stare
The one-eyed giant's gaze of gold.

We, too, our own resources hold
And with them make clothes to wear
In the world of our own earth's fold.

Plant-trapped, the life that eyeball rolled
Has brought us food and life to spare.
The one-eyed giant's gaze of gold

Has broken patterns, made us bold
To climb from sea to sky and dare,
In the world of our own earth's fold
The one-eyed giant's gaze of gold.

How Can I Say . . . ?

How can I say what means the most in me
And talk the talk which academics use?
There's no freshness in vocabulary

Which puts a cause above adversity;
The spring of living action is abuse.
How can I say what means the most to me

Without after-labels that must set free
The present pain which psychic life renews?
There's no freshness in vocabulary;

When a meaning's given, longevity
Relegates the matter to an abstruse.
How can I say what means the most to me

When everywhere around, fluidity
Of movement is live energy diffuse?
There's no freshness in vocabulary

Where motion rules and rationality
Is but a counter-poise, a pale excuse.
How can I say what means the most in me?
There's no freshness in vocabulary.

Black And White

In the mind-world whose perfections
Do not depend on laws
Any element gives reflections
Too light and swift for cause.

In case you question what is right,
Answers are more than one
And all depend on where is light
When moving rays have gone.

Though what we say can cover truth
As clothes can cover skin
The air we breathe may hold no proof
There's anything within.

In simple words where joy and grief
Are nuts too hard to crack
Let's say: "Life's a tree. In each leaf
Black is white, white is black."

Two Sculptures

I viewed two sculptures in Vancouver. One was
in the Buddhist temple, the other in the International
Airport. I do not know who designed the first; Bill
Reid of the Haida Gwai made the second.

Around each was grouped a culture's psyche.
    Buddhism
showed at least ten varied Buddhas whose poses
were all unity. Bill Reid's subject was outside
ungrouped totemic animals, each looking outward,
bewildered, and alone.

One thing struck me. There was marked difference
    in colours.
Though both designs looked identical,
the Buddhist priest who made one group had eyes
for surface gold. Inside our darker age,
Bill Reid's bronze saw black.

Alone In A Forest

Alone in a forest of almost night
I raise my head, hoping to catch the spark
Of other eyes that long for eerie light
In the unharvested kernels of dark.

Alone in a forest that's almost dead
I lift myself up and I look around,
Hoping against hope the ears in my head
Can gather at least a patter of sound.

Alone in a forest that's much too still
I play a dummy's part and gaze askance,
Trying to hear new-music's moving thrill,
The semi-silence of a leaf's green dance.

Comma Butterfly

This insect here behind this pane
Was once a living butterfly
But now it cannot even fly
Nor take a sip from maple sap again.

I know, despite life's mighty reign,
All things die, but it was my pride
Which smothered it in cyanide
And gave it poison, also pain.

So now I keep it on the shelf . . .
Though once when life was daily dull
I thought to own what's beautiful
Forever and just by myself.

At Times Sometimes

I

At times sometimes when you probe with your mind
For what it is which you remember there
The chances are your brain will sometimes find
Just a few words to make your body care
So much they bring tears to your empty eye;
But where they come from you'll not know why.

II

At times sometimes you're apt to run into
People you'd lived with in busy years
But whom in fact you never really knew.
From one of these I learned my friendly tears
For her lack of memory of the past
Delighted her. She was alone at last.

Girls

In years when I grew up most boys were shy
When close to their own-age girl company.
It made them nervous though they knew not why
But since that was the way, they let it be.

Though girls were dumb, yet as the years went by
Few of them went off to a nunnery.
Most stood up to boys, looked them in the eye,
Became the mothers of posterity.

Though a state they felt after a long trip
Grew sacred like the vows of a sacristy,
They would often stare at a starlit sky
And long for a light they would never see.

By this we know, no matter where we look,
Men and women are words in the same book.

Wherever I Watch . . .

Wherever I watch a Ferris wheel fly
Before it pauses in a lofty spot
The contrast then between the earth and sky
Makes me question one question that I've got.

How many miles now as the years unfold
Have I sped through space since my day of birth
And yet have not felt around me the hold
Of the quiet arms of our mother earth?

Perhaps it's best to stop all questionings.
Maybe the hows and whys of ways we miss
Belong so well they are family things
So close there's no need to give them notice.

To Form Sweet Notes

To form sweet notes, unlike the singing birds
That chorus in the ways where nature went,
A brain must choose appropriate words
And find for them a sounding instrument.

To form sweet notes, the players must
Be taught by teachers who will teach them well.
They also need an audience whom they trust
That their best playing can a crowd compel.

When this song was ended, it did sound good.
Both pitch and rhythm were a sheer delight.
The crowd clapped hands. It never understood
The nonsense of a one-man copyright.

Perhaps Too Fortunate, The Worm

Perhaps too fortunate the worm
Required no urge to change its form.
It surely knew that nature meant
It to fit its environment,
For everywhere its lot was flung
It kept the contours of a tongue.
Down its whole length sense-feeling's glue
Made it seem priapic, too.
It did not need a tooth to bite
In an earth made for appetite.

Happy because it lacked a sky
Without the germs of brain and eye,
It knew neither god nor devil
Made the spores of good and evil.

Film Review: The Fast Runner

Whenever a sex-fire's lit
Human extremes clash and meet.
Even in igloos the Inuit
Are harried by blood-heat.

But we who lack such sinning
Watch both hate and tenderness
From a troubled beginning
To an end in nakedness.

But it does give examples
Of what real humans need
With excellent samples
Of endurance and speed.

Two Fables

Trying to salvage from wrecked memory
By scanning encyclopedias
For titles whose names had long escaped me
I had the good luck today to find two,
The Wild Ass's Skin, The Deformed Transformed,
Balzac's novel and Lord Byron's poem.

Both of them were fables; both were long my guides.
Balzac said, "You must pay for what you do."
And Byron, "Do. Only energy's real."
I now can add two more names to the list
Of works that helped to make me what I am.
The value of the result I still don't know.

Henry Adams At Chartres

Word-sophisticated, with facts to gnaw,
At Chartres, although his vision was unclear
Henry Adams felt some awe. His mind was near
Enough to feel the faith he almost saw.

It gave him theory, or at least its ground.
This dying world beneath its mystery
Epitomized the Virgin's history.
Mary's strength was the key element found.

But what faith he had in a cathedral
He could not keep. He knew that Norman men
Had gambled on her holiness and when
There was scant payment they let her fall.

At the first World's Fair in Chicago
When America's new god caught his eye
He knew then that a goddess, too, must die
To feed a hungry, soulless dynamo.

The Magic Tree

Through Winter, Summer, Fall, and Spring
Above the world that blind men see
Strong faith-winds blow, seed-blossoming
To make indeed a magic tree.

Once grown, its parts display their gifts.
For these they struggle night and day.
The solid trunk which holds them shifts
Whenever time turns green to grey.

So small is faith each word's a leaf.
No matter what the seasons are
It christens joy and covers grief
And for its labours bears no scar.

Its beauty, though, is sheer delight
To an uneducated eye.
In all times when the air is light
It can leave our own dark world and fly.

Although it speaks too much of sin
With saintly grace for one and all
The world's best sap it can't put in.
It knows not "will be" nor "recall".

II.
Incidentals

Carmen

Ere it could spin the sweet tune of her days
The frail disk broke. Death's needle pierced too strong.
But still in memory her record plays . . .
It keeps alive the Latin word for song.

A Tribute

In translation a line from Hesiod
More beautiful than human minds can hold
Reads like the best gift of a rural god:
"The apple tree, the singing, and the gold."

The Dress

This dress is scarcely worn, the shape of grace
Is here, but no one's left to put it on.
What's missing in the emptiness of space,
Is the loveliness which filled it. It is gone.

A Poem Is A Saw

A poem is a saw whose sharp teeth shave
Through logs that many knots have burled
Where written words can move a lathe
And make it turn a better world.

In The Mad World

In the mad world we want too much to reach
A jest or a gesture can build a wall.
So strong with us is the power of speech
I often think we don't need hands at all.

Once We Watched . . .

Once we watched two mantis mate.
As one of these the other slew
I thought I heard my sweetheart state:
"Darling, I could eat you, too!"

Seven Words

Seven words which I could not ever find
Are back by miracle inside my mind
I write these down since memory is lame:
"Childe Roland to the dark tower came."

I've Written Poems

I've written poems, a small amount,
To raise above a world that seems;
And in the land of written dreams
Where words are wealth I hope they count.

Reflections

An ape-man glimpsed a humid mask of grace
Which—mistaking features for god's real face—
He wore. Beside the water, god looked on.
Each thought the other was its reflection

To A Friend

Although I found his inner life was gold
Both thought and feeling were too far apart.
I'd join the two. But could one body hold
Inside one flesh that vibrant head and heart?

Augustine

Whenever he thought of divinity
Saint Augustine's trinity was not odd.
With cloth he owned from is, was, and will be
He together wove one coat to fit one god.

There were three gifts that made his natal dower:
A sex-starved mother's love discovered young,
A Roman father's view of city power,
And a smooth politician's canny tongue.

Harriet Beecher Stowe

In Uncle Tom her love of freedom shone.
Blacks she wrote of made the north white world weep.
Why in the great highland-clan expulsion
Instead of tribesmen did she prefer sheep?

Inside The Hollow Heart

Inside the hollow heart of giant wood
Whose silence played life's coda of full rest
Still I stand and meditate. It is good
To heed the quiet air of Nature's best.

Divisive Walls

Divisive walls that men live in
Have rifts through which they fear to pass.
I'd prefer mind-worlds fused so thin
I'd never know the walls were glass.

DE SADE

Unless we know on what both good and bad
Depend, we cannot all the truth unseal.
Would Count de Sade have been the same de Sade
If he had not been put in the Bastille?

FIRST TIME

In Exeter, the night was wild.
I listened, looked, and stood
Where buzzing wasps white clouds defiled
With streaks more black than blood.

It brought one instant when I could
Not let the world avail.
The soul in me realized for good
Both sky and earth can fail.

We Dig Beneath

We dig beneath this earth of blackness which
Holds oil and diamonds, precious pearls and coal.
Are steals like these that make us all too rich
Enough to change the whiteness of our soul?

The Work Ethic

Use of strength which makes muscles sound
Applies as well to thought.
What will not move itself is bound
In time to die of rot.

The Dwarf Bonsai

In China, though its leaves are bare
And its rough trunk is sere and dry,
A plethora of loving care
Is given to the dwarf bonsai.

A Subject For Shame

It was a subject for shame
To all who are free,
But I've forgotten the name
And the nationality
Of the boy who cried "Canada!"
With his last breath
As men from our army
Beat him to death.

On The Beach

. . . gently the wind's touch
washes the sleeping sea; your hand
moves over my skin.

If Brainless Apes

If brainless apes went on a crazy blast
Completely drunk inside their killing spree
Could deeds like theirs justify the past
Which marred the earth's most brutal century?

Although The Past . . .

Although the past my body cast away
Will not now in the flesh return to me,
My mind has never lost the will to pay
The debt love owes to possibility.
Thank God, it has not lost its memory!

Without A Sound

The coral's speech is life. With it I agree.
And what it says, defying time and tide,
Is "You cannot completely prison me."
I hear it as it sips our cyanide.

Assessment

In a wind too loud for thunder
The freeze of age our peace assaults.
What god has planted states, I wonder,
On such hard volcanic faults?

Still on poor earth's rich soil of woe
Where airy thoughts can scarce stay green
Some wise men try to make fruit grow
In Harper's thorny magazine.

The World I Live In

The world I live in pretends it's moral
But greed is its morality.
When the earth looks grim I think of coral—
The Sydney Carton of the sea.

Now I Am Old . . .

Now I am old my face looks very odd
As my withered skin makes my eyes complain
About the changes that are there. Thank God,
I cannot see the wrinkles on my brain.

Base-Lines On Marriage

Through marriage is still called a sacrament
Some worshippers find its rites a task:
Too many know that time's a too-long Lent
Where rage's luxury can rip off a mask.

Noise

The germs of noise which this vile era sucks
Have stinking sounds that make all flesh recoil.
Children catch them. The worst are sitting trucks
Which howl in giant glee as they guzzle oil.

Our Curt Concern

Our curt concern for bad and good
Obscures the life we fear to lose.
This world around's a multitude
Where we don't know enough to choose.

I, Unborn . . .

I, unborn, felt no happiness because
My mother carried me in her young prime.
As months went by the embryo I was
Was world-chained to movement, space, and time.

Dilemma

When now so many firms are fake
And cruel mean lies are often told
How can I tell the wealth I make
Is real or only fairy gold?

Once The Pebbles On The Beach

Once the pebbles on the beach were dull,
Rough, and mixed up with slime beside.
When smooth whiteness made them beautiful
The architects were wind and tide.

The Red Rose

That fall, after my first wife died,
In the yard beyond the bedroom
A red rose bitter frost defied
To keep one solitary bloom.

It struggled hard and stayed quite tough
Until long past December snows.
The day it died was grim enough
To make all poetry turn prose.

An Author's Name

An author's name to credit poetry
Is wrong. Poetry is a mass uniting.
Minds that were, that are, minds that will be
Are live things that join to make one writing.

When Chance Rage

When chance rage broke the sacred ground,
Then Cain grew wroth and Abel died.
Since this not even God has found
An answer to such fratricide.

The Broad Dark Street

The broad dark street was rife with revelry.
A black cat ignored the scene.
Although the moon was full, it did not see
Its role in Hallowe'en.

As Far As Answers Go

As far as answers go, words with most sense
Are "yes" and "no" and "wrong" and "right",
But since my nature won't stand suspense
What I hate most has always been "I might".

Earth-Play (For Anti-Environmentalists)

One time an actor-god,
Tired of Aggripina,
Erased a mother-part
Which is now called Gaia.

But Earth, whose deeds sometimes
Can begin with zero.
Still lets her killer-stars
Play the part of Nero.

Although Words . . .

Although words are short and curt
To celebrate past love
I find that some verses hurt
For what they remind me of.

The Sting

When the C.I.A. applied its screw
It found what most men thought they knew:
"Wheelers and dealers
Can be squealers, too."

Wind And Rain

Wind and rain can make one weather
Its full creation form
As yin and yang together
Build up a mighty storm.

Brotherhood

Impulsively I struck a fly's black skin
Until the force of my blow made it break.
Some organs were out and some were in.
The fact is, I did not even try to make
Repairs but left it alone to ache
Or die as Christians might do with a snake.

The Poetry Of Energy

The poetry of energy
Is much more than you and me.
If pulses through earth's ceiling
And rages under sea,
But the words we use to catch
Quicksilver feeling
Are far too slow to match.

When I Re-Read My Poems . . .

When I re-read my poems I find
Inside a single countenance
Each is the love-child of one mind
And a different circumstance
Which is why I often wonder
How much and to how long degree
A bard like me should lie under
So many Muses' lechery.

Exposed Now To A Light . . .

Exposed now to a light I did not know
Was in me, the world caught me by surprise,
Embracing my whole being with a glow
That came inherent out of laser eyes.

It did not make my own desire grow
To find in other nerves a rare new bliss.
Enough it was for me to take and owe
Forever to have had a joy like this.

Grammar Is Mainly Hit Or Miss

Grammar is mainly hit or miss
But two short words tell us where one is at.
A thing which is ours we have to name "this",
But if it is theirs, we can call it "that".

The Lord Of The Rings

The Lord of the Rings provided for all
The taste of full-grown bloody girls and boys
The crude ingredients of a carnival.
As men, like flies, buzzed out their brainless noise
They made the breath they wasted seem to be
Their main donation to this century.

Taste

In unity of taste Nature is no saint.
She fits unfitted things in a single class
And human hands as well have learned to paint
A living fish inside a sea of glass.

Yet time has power to heal mistakes somehow
That once jarred connoisseurs who hate grotesque,
And few there are who notice this now
A thornless rose upon a polished desk.

The Things Which Tell Me

The things which tell me what I am
But don't quite know how to express
Are not quite true and not quite sham;
Confusion covers nakedness.

The debt I owe posterity
Is that it made the man you know;
Minds I never met created me
And modern stylings hide their show.

Fear

There's a fear in you and me,
A deep discord which makes
Our bodies cringe at beauty
That's shaped like snakes.

Is it because brains must know
Despite all they perform
That the master of earth's flow
Remains the worm?

Automatic Responses

Automatic responses and not thought
Rule most decisions that we make today;
When rank is honoured and people are not
No need for judgement to get in the way.

Once I Fashioned Verse

Once I fashioned verse critics thought was good
And mailed it to my Muse who in a letter
Wrote back, "You haven't done the best you could.
Destroy this now. After that write better."

III.
(Arranged from the French)

HERODIAS
(Théodore de Banville)

Like waters of Jordan her eyes are clear.
The heavy necklace and pendants she wears
Look sweeter than grapes the wine trellis bears
And the wood-rose is convinced of her sneer.

She frolics and laughs with a playful air,
Letting her youth display each fine marvel,
Her red lips and teeth that can parallel
In whiteness the lilies of the parterre.

Watch her coming, the young queen striding bold!
A black page lifts up her robe to unfold
The whole corridor voluptuously.

From her fingers, rubies, sapphires, amethyst,
Resplendent gleam as on a gold plate she
Bears the bleeding head of John the Baptist.

To A Passer-By
(Charles Baudelaire)

Around me I hear harsh street-noises bray.
Slim, tall, and in majestic mourning, grand
A woman went her way. Her rhythmic hand
Made festoon and hem deftly rise and sway;

Noble-limbed and statuesque in measure.
And my eyes drank, twisted in outlandish pain,
Twin pulses from her gathered hurricane,
Appealing softness and killing pleasure.

Lightning flash . . . darkness. O fleeting beauty
Whose look suddenly gives me a new birth.
Shall I see only in eternity

You too late, far off! Maybe not on earth?
For, lost myself, I know not where you flew,
O you I would have loved (you knew that, too)

Windows
(Charles Baudelaire)

One who looks from outside through an open window,
    never sees
As many things as one who looks through a closed
    window.
There is no object more profound, more mysterious,
More fecund, more gloomy, more dazzling than a
Window lit by a candle. What we can see in sunlight
Is always less interesting than what goes on behind a
Window. Inside this black or white life lives,
Life dreams, life suffers.

Beyond roof-waves, I perceive a mature woman, already
Wrinkled, poor, always bent over something, and
    who never
Goes out. With her countenance, with her dress,
    with her
Movement, with almost nothing, I recreate that
    woman's
Story, or rather her legend, and some times I recall
    her to
Myself weeping.

If she had been a poor old man, I would have
Recreated her easily.

I go to bed, proud to have lived and suffered in others
Than myself.

Maybe you will ask me: "Are you sure this story
Can be true?" What does reality outside me
Matter, if it helps me to live, to feel that I
Am and what I am?

In Brown Limbs . . .
(Emile Blémont)

In brown limbs, the breeze goes crazy,
The morning yet whitens the lawn;
Dawn's here; everything is rosy;
The palace to odours has gone.

Heaven's air mixes the foliage
Of the birds and fountains which sing;
Earth and water blossoms engage
The best of their homage to Spring.

O the tremble of willow leaves,
Summer's gold-end, your prime delight
Snow that to a poet's heart cleaves;
Flowers where the pear trees are white.

Reflection
(Joë Bousquet)

Around the world there moves a sea
The tree and its shadow combine
Unknown hands write beautifully
Misdeeds which in deep water shine.

A Bird
(René Char)

A bird sings live simplicity.
An earth-flower on an earth-twig.
It fills our hells at once with glee.

The wind begins its suffering
And all the stars grow bright and big.

O fools, to dash about, trying
To find such deep fatality!

Landscape

(Robert Desnos)

I dreamed of love. I still love, but that love
Is only a lilac-and-rose bouquet
Filling with its perfume a woodland way
Where flame is born from paths they cannot move.

I dream of love. I still love, but that love
Is only this storm whose flash interposes
House woodsheds, confesses, decomposes,
Lights up the good-byes which all cross-roads prove.

It's sand burning in dark under my feet.
No dictionaries can translate these thoughts,
Cloud covers the sky, foam burdens the sea.

Growing old, everything turns bright and straight.
Boulevards without names, cards without knots.
I feel stiffen now both landscape and me.

Nothing Alarms Me More
(Paul Éluard)

Nothing alarms me more than the lull I see
Of a face that sleeps cold;
Your dream is an Egypt and you are a mummy
With its stiff mask of gold.

When your gaze goes under that rich purview
Of a Queen dying there,
Will love's darkness break as it repaints you
Like a black embalmer?

Abandon, my queen, my wild duck, the place,
Seas where centuries drown;
Rise up, floating on top, get back your face
That now sinks up and down.

Forbidden
(Léonard Forest)

if there were, in the depth of me, a forbidden
    mountain
would i ask you to go there, my love
would i ask you to go there?

you know my beeches, my back-meadows,
my dark images, my hard-to-suit bay;
you know the blue chameleon that glows,
my wave that will root in dreams of noonday.

if there were, in the depths of me, a forbidden
    mountain,
would i ask you to go there, my love
would i ask you to go there?

you know my images of you, ecstasies
woven of silk and gold, the velvet refrain
of a so-light dance under the skies,
the hot-lands you dream of against the grain.

if there were, in the depth of me, a forbidden
    mountain
would i ask you to go there, my love,
would i ask you to go there?

you know the fire that sleeps inside me,
the smell of burning time, and the green glare
of spruce offering; you feel suddenly
the joy-cloud to be discovered there.

if there were, in the depth of me, a forbidden
    mountain,
would i ask you to go there, my love,
would i ask you to go there?

you know your inventions, a swirling flow
of half-secrets; your flight the triple flow
of faithfulness and you would truly know
how to love the gifts with humble pride.

you know my bed of absence, the slow prey
that prowls my land, accomplice even,
my night flights, the solitary affray,
the naked breath crushed out twixt earth and heaven.

if there were, in the depth of me, a forbidden
    mountain,
would i ask you to go there, my love,
would i ask you to go there?

you know your gardens, thrush, free from all fear
unpunished, you dance in the sunlit strand
where now is. i and tomorrow are peers
of the mute ebb and flow around the island.

if there were, in the depth of me, a forbidden
    mountain,
would i ask you to go there, my love,
would i ask you to go there?

An Unending Song
(Léonard Forest)

when i went abroad to roam
along with sweet-hearts splendid,
three girls i had taken home
after my tour was ended.
ah, how high is memory,
ah, how sad is my story.

        a song's egg-like style,
        joy like a peach-crop,
        and a brand new smile,
        a love nothing can stop.

there where sea-meadows burst
i found the first one dear,
though i ate summer first,
next came the rest of the year,
how great the thought which gripped my love,
how sad my heart empty of love.

> a song's egg-like style,
> joy like a peach-crop,
> and a brand new smile,
> a love nothing can stop.

inside the mountain's shadow
i found a second love,
how divine i could bestow
all the joys i wove,
but from what height did she smother
my company for another!

> a song's egg-like style,
> joy like a peach-crop,
> and a brand new smile,
> a love nothing can stop.

on the prairie i found Helene,
most beautiful of the three
i made no advances then,
without appeal she conquered me.
what has happened to passion at all
when its growth becomes laughable!

        a song's egg-like style,
        joy like a peach-crop,
        and a brand new smile,
        a love nothing can stop.

on my tour three prisoners
languish in tenderness.
moved, i hear their prayers
and their kind promises.
tonight, weary, i'll quit my turn.
i'll fall alone and, loveless, learn.

        a song's egg-like style,
        joy like a peach-crop,
        and a brand new smile,
        a love nothing can stop.

Sonnet
(Émile Goudreau)

When I shall rest in the grave, unmoving,
Having around me the eternal blur
When my limbs have lost their power to stir
And my hollow eyes a look that's sparkling.

This being I was, this poor fragile thing,
Will sleep forgotten and there ossify
Forever underneath a cloudy sky
Where nothing more from that clay couch will spring.

But you will still be beauty forever
Beyond common death, inside tradition:
Being my soul, your body cannot die!

On my tomb when nights for love will draw on
And that woman's ghost for a long time draws by,
You'll wake yourself, Beauty's skeleton lover.

Léda

(Jean Lahor)

To the trembling swan who offers her bliss
She gives her lusty body mindlessly.
Immortals will be both of this mute kiss
And on this side Helen's form will come to be.

Through the strong sparks in dark mysterious odds
Always this way stupid matter comes and
With a mindless woman procreates Gods
Without guessing where so much light could land.

The Prairie

(Charles Leconte de Lisle)

On the huge prairie, a sea with no strands,
Surges of moving grass minus horizons,
Hundreds of red horsemen in savage bands
Harrying a wild torrent of bisons.

Eagle-plumes on brow and from face to breast
Streaked vermilion; bow at fist, quiver along
Kidneys, tied by a thin dark thong,
Giving lowing beasts a desperate test.

Urged by barbed-wire jerks gashing their sides
The horsy bulls gallop, bellowing loud,
And the tangles between their grassy strides
Are mingled with spit and blood in a cloud.

The mass deepens, tangling hair now growing.
Erasing wounds, death, and dwarfed chaparral,
Freeing rocks, water-courses, on-going
Amid agonizing rales that appall.

Far-off behind them but glued to their spoor
The desert's white wolves in silence follow
With their tongues hanging out; staring and poor,
They flash with desire their eye's sharpest glow.

Then all this mass it seems cannot reform;
Bellows, shouts, wolves, cowboys outside their grounds
In a trice, like a sudden thunder-storm,
Revolve, fly, ebb and shy by leaps and bounds.

Pegasus

(Pierre Louÿs)

With his four pure feet on earth flashing bright
The fabled beast is torn. His virgin chest
That by no man nor god can be harnessed
Explodes in a lively mysterious flight.

He soars, and the sparse mane in haloed light
Of a falling horse makes an immortal star
That glitters in the dark gold sky like far
Orion in the frost of Eola's night.

As in times when spirits free in their deeds
Drank from the sacred flood, under boots even,
The sidereal cavalcades' illusion,

The Poets in mourning for their ruined creeds
Still almost imagine their hand-grips on
The white stallion bounding in forbidden heaven.

Song

(Jean Moréas)

We walked over flowers at the side of the road
And the Fall wind disturbed them as strongly again.

The mail-coach upset the cross at the side of the road.
It had truly rotted so much as that again.

The idiot (you know) is dead at the side of the road
And no one who is there will cry for him again.

The Deep Life
(Anna de Noailles)

To be nature as a human-tree stands,
Putting out its desires like a deep foliage
And sensing, through quiet night and storm-rage,
The universal sap flowing through its hands!

Living, having the sun's rays gleam on one's face,
Drinking tears of joy and grief, fresh caught
And quickly swallowed down. These, piping hot,
Create a human dish in time and space.

Feeling air, fire and blood in its live heart,
Swirling as if it were wind-moving soil;
It rises to the reel, bends on recoil
Between day-rise and shadows which depart.

Like a royal evening, cherry-red,
That lets its rose heart colour flame and tide
And, like clear dawn resting on a hillside,
There is a dream-soul at world-edge seated.

The Four Elements
(Géo Norge)

Earth Earth is good to eat,
People, beasts who spree!
You'll then be quiet
Very dreadfully.

Water Drunk, all waters flow
From seas resonant
And the heart says: O
My thirst I still want.

Fire Sole fire, sole flame.
It's the fire of hell
Knows how to boil soul
And the flesh as well

Air Here's infinite space
In which pride can bloom.
This is desire's place
Inside your bedroom.

Late In Life
(Pierre Reverdy)

I am hard
I am tender
                And I've wasted my time
                Dreaming without sleeping
                Sleeping while marching
Everywhere I went
I found I was not there
I am no where
Except vanity
But I carry hidden in the top of my gut
At the spot where thunder has struck too often
A heart where every word has left its bruise
And from which my life drained at the least
    movement.

Privilege
(Claude Serret)

A bird going by
A bird on the bough

A star that's unknown
A star to be known

And the name of an hour
Love that gave it a name

Swallow or blue-tit
Marguerite or jonquil

I seek them and find
I find them and sing

Lovely bird lovely star
We sing to please them.

THE POETRY OF THE STREET
(Marcel Thiry)

The poetry of the street is welcome
After this too long a day
As it once was when sweet balm
Calmed love and soul away.

Do not seek other images or
Ask pardon for what's left for you where
The street just sits calmly there
After too much glare, people, and uproar.

Content your self tonight. Love like brethren
Weary pavements and tired horses. Then
Recontent yourself, loving their echoings
Go, go, don't try to rhyme happy things!

SILENT, SLEEK, AND PERFECTLY . . .
(Jean Tortel)

Silent, sleek and perfectly
Round. Such is sunlight
Far from Winter,
An abstract view.

No blazing but sunset orange
Above the platanes
Heralding nothing.

No thunder-storm.

Hardly clear at day-noon
Sky's paleness makes up its mind
In whatever blue casts no shadow.

It is not the deep and green blue
Colour of a body.

Pomegranates
(Paul Valéry)

Pomegranates half set free
Yielding to your seeds' excess
I think I see brow's noblesse
Bursting with discovery

If the suns that made you be,
O pomegranates now ajar,
Gave you pride for what you are
To crack your walls of ruby,

And what if your gold bark wakes
At the call of a sun-beam
And a red gem of juice break?

That luminous rapture
Is making my soul dream
Of its secret structure.

The Cry
(Émile Verhaeren)

Near a desert pond where brown water slumbers sure
A twilight ray drops a glow on a reed's summit;
A cry is heard, the distressed cry of a linnet,
A cry on the infinite plain ruined and poor.

How feeble and frail it is, how timid and drawn!
And how with sadness it drops and listens and heeds.
How it repeats itself. On its way through the reeds
It sinks and loses itself in the still horizon!

And how it marks down time by its rattling tempos,
And how, by its accents pathetically weak
And in its echoes also languishing and sick,
It is preening itself for its vespered woes!

Sometimes it is so mild we cannot catch its breaths.
Less still, all the same, it drones tirelessly on
The obscure and sad goodbye of a sane life gone
Its song celebrates the poor dead and their mean deaths.

The death of flowers, the death of insects,
    the sweet loss
Of wings, and of plant-stalks, and perfumes
    that hover
There reign in memory of flights which are over
And that lie hidden in the grass and in the moss.

The Sky Is, Over The Roof
(Paul Verlaine)

The sky is, over the roof
So blue, so calm!
A tree is, over the roof
Cradling its palm.

The clock we see in the sky
Looks soft and faint.
A bird we see in the tree
Sings his complaint

My God, my God, life's poise there
Is simple peace.
That quiet noise we hear is
The town's release.

What have you made, O you there,
Weeping in truth,
Tell me, what have you made there
Out of your youth?

On The Earth . . .

(André Ferdinand Hérold)

On the earth the snow is falling.
On the earth the shadow is falling.

Where have all the dry leaves gone?
Even the dry leaves are dead,
And now the snow and the shadow are falling.
We would speak of bad angels.

We would speak of bad angels colliding,
Of rusted hammers against the doors,
Of angels who kill us with gentle suffering.
And, at the horizon, and clouds, trailing . . .

The houses are closed like somber tombs,
And, everywhere, snow and shadow are falling.

AGMV Marquis
MEMBER OF SCABRINI MEDIA
Quebec, Canada
2003